BILL PAYMENT ORGANIZER

This book belongs to:

_____

_____

_____

BILL PAYMENT  ORGANIZER

YEAR: ....   **MONTH:** ....

PAID	BILL	DUE DATE	AMOUNT DUE	AMOUNT PAID	UNPAID BALANCE	NOTES
○						
○						
○						
○						
○						
○						
○						
○						
○						
○						
○						
○						
○						
○						
○						
○						
○						
○						
○						
○						
○						
○						
○						
○						
TOTAL						

NOTES: _____

_____

_____

BILL PAYMENT ORGANIZER

YEAR: .... **MONTH:** ....

PAID	BILL	DUE DATE	AMOUNT DUE	AMOUNT PAID	UNPAID BALANCE	NOTES
◯						
◯						
◯						
◯						
◯						
◯						
◯						
◯						
◯						
◯						
◯						
◯						
◯						
◯						
◯						
◯						
◯						
◯						
◯						
◯						
◯						
◯						
◯						
◯						
TOTAL						

NOTES: ....

....

....

BILL PAYMENT  ORGANIZER

YEAR: ....   **MONTH:** ....

PAID	BILL	DUE DATE	AMOUNT DUE	AMOUNT PAID	UNPAID BALANCE	NOTES
○						
○						
○						
○						
○						
○						
○						
○						
○						
○						
○						
○						
○						
○						
○						
○						
○						
○						
○						
○						
○						
○						
○						
○						
TOTAL						

NOTES: _____

_____

_____

BILL PAYMENT  ORGANIZER

YEAR: .... MONTH: ....

PAID	BILL	DUE DATE	AMOUNT DUE	AMOUNT PAID	UNPAID BALANCE	NOTES
○						
○						
○						
○						
○						
○						
○						
○						
○						
○						
○						
○						
○						
○						
○						
○						
○						
○						
○						
○						
○						
○						
○						
○						
TOTAL						

NOTES: _____

_____

_____

BILL PAYMENT  ORGANIZER

YEAR: .... **MONTH:** ....

PAID	BILL	DUE DATE	AMOUNT DUE	AMOUNT PAID	UNPAID BALANCE	NOTES
○						
○						
○						
○						
○						
○						
○						
○						
○						
○						
○						
○						
○						
○						
○						
○						
○						
○						
○						
○						
○						
○						
○						
○						
TOTAL						

NOTES: _____

_____

_____

BILL PAYMENT  ORGANIZER

YEAR: .... **MONTH:** ....

PAID	BILL	DUE DATE	AMOUNT DUE	AMOUNT PAID	UNPAID BALANCE	NOTES
○						
○						
○						
○						
○						
○						
○						
○						
○						
○						
○						
○						
○						
○						
○						
○						
○						
○						
○						
○						
○						
○						
○						
○						
TOTAL						

NOTES: _____

_____

_____

BILL PAYMENT  ORGANIZER

YEAR: ....   **MONTH:** ....

PAID	BILL	DUE DATE	AMOUNT DUE	AMOUNT PAID	UNPAID BALANCE	NOTES
○						
○						
○						
○						
○						
○						
○						
○						
○						
○						
○						
○						
○						
○						
○						
○						
○						
○						
○						
○						
○						
○						
○						
○						
TOTAL						

NOTES: _____

_____

_____

BILL PAYMENT ORGANIZER

YEAR: ....   MONTH: ....

PAID	BILL	DUE DATE	AMOUNT DUE	AMOUNT PAID	UNPAID BALANCE	NOTES
○						
○						
○						
○						
○						
○						
○						
○						
○						
○						
○						
○						
○						
○						
○						
○						
○						
○						
○						
○						
○						
○						
○						
TOTAL						

NOTES: _____

_____

_____

BILL PAYMENT ORGANIZER

YEAR: ....   MONTH: ....

PAID	BILL	DUE DATE	AMOUNT DUE	AMOUNT PAID	UNPAID BALANCE	NOTES
○						
○						
○						
○						
○						
○						
○						
○						
○						
○						
○						
○						
○						
○						
○						
○						
○						
○						
○						
○						
○						
○						
○						
TOTAL						

NOTES: _____

_____

_____

BILL PAYMENT  ORGANIZER

YEAR: ....   MONTH: ....

PAID	BILL	DUE DATE	AMOUNT DUE	AMOUNT PAID	UNPAID BALANCE	NOTES
○						
○						
○						
○						
○						
○						
○						
○						
○						
○						
○						
○						
○						
○						
○						
○						
○						
○						
○						
○						
○						
○						
○						
○						
TOTAL						

NOTES: _____

_____

_____

BILL PAYMENT  ORGANIZER

YEAR: ....   **MONTH:** ....

PAID	BILL	DUE DATE	AMOUNT DUE	AMOUNT PAID	UNPAID BALANCE	NOTES
◯						
◯						
◯						
◯						
◯						
◯						
◯						
◯						
◯						
◯						
◯						
◯						
◯						
◯						
◯						
◯						
◯						
◯						
◯						
◯						
◯						
◯						
◯						
TOTAL						

NOTES: _____

_____

_____

BILL PAYMENT  ORGANIZER

YEAR: .... **MONTH:** ....

PAID	BILL	DUE DATE	AMOUNT DUE	AMOUNT PAID	UNPAID BALANCE	NOTES
○						
○						
○						
○						
○						
○						
○						
○						
○						
○						
○						
○						
○						
○						
○						
○						
○						
○						
○						
○						
○						
○						
○						
○						
○						
TOTAL						

NOTES: _____

_____

_____

BILL PAYMENT  ORGANIZER

YEAR: .... MONTH: ....

PAID	BILL	DUE DATE	AMOUNT DUE	AMOUNT PAID	UNPAID BALANCE	NOTES
○						
○						
○						
○						
○						
○						
○						
○						
○						
○						
○						
○						
○						
○						
○						
○						
○						
○						
○						
○						
○						
○						
○						
○						
○						
TOTAL						

NOTES: _____

_____

_____

BILL PAYMENT  ORGANIZER

YEAR: ....   **MONTH:** ....

PAID	BILL	DUE DATE	AMOUNT DUE	AMOUNT PAID	UNPAID BALANCE	NOTES
○						
○						
○						
○						
○						
○						
○						
○						
○						
○						
○						
○						
○						
○						
○						
○						
○						
○						
○						
○						
○						
○						
○						
○						
TOTAL						

NOTES: _____

_____

_____

BILL PAYMENT  ORGANIZER

YEAR: ....   MONTH: ....

PAID	BILL	DUE DATE	AMOUNT DUE	AMOUNT PAID	UNPAID BALANCE	NOTES
○						
○						
○						
○						
○						
○						
○						
○						
○						
○						
○						
○						
○						
○						
○						
○						
○						
○						
○						
○						
○						
○						
○						
○						
TOTAL						

NOTES: _____

_____

_____

BILL PAYMENT  ORGANIZER

YEAR: ....   **MONTH:** ....

PAID	BILL	DUE DATE	AMOUNT DUE	AMOUNT PAID	UNPAID BALANCE	NOTES
○						
○						
○						
○						
○						
○						
○						
○						
○						
○						
○						
○						
○						
○						
○						
○						
○						
○						
○						
○						
○						
○						
○						
○						
TOTAL						

NOTES: _____

_____

_____

BILL PAYMENT  ORGANIZER

YEAR: .... MONTH: ....

PAID	BILL	DUE DATE	AMOUNT DUE	AMOUNT PAID	UNPAID BALANCE	NOTES
○						
○						
○						
○						
○						
○						
○						
○						
○						
○						
○						
○						
○						
○						
○						
○						
○						
○						
○						
○						
○						
○						
○						
○						
TOTAL						

NOTES: _____

_____

_____

BILL PAYMENT  ORGANIZER

YEAR: ....   MONTH: ....

PAID	BILL	DUE DATE	AMOUNT DUE	AMOUNT PAID	UNPAID BALANCE	NOTES
○						
○						
○						
○						
○						
○						
○						
○						
○						
○						
○						
○						
○						
○						
○						
○						
○						
○						
○						
○						
○						
○						
○						
○						
TOTAL						

NOTES: _____

_____

_____

BILL PAYMENT  ORGANIZER

YEAR: ....   MONTH: ....

PAID	BILL	DUE DATE	AMOUNT DUE	AMOUNT PAID	UNPAID BALANCE	NOTES
○						
○						
○						
○						
○						
○						
○						
○						
○						
○						
○						
○						
○						
○						
○						
○						
○						
○						
○						
○						
○						
○						
○						
○						
TOTAL						

NOTES: _____

_____

BILL PAYMENT ORGANIZER

YEAR: .... MONTH: ....

PAID	BILL	DUE DATE	AMOUNT DUE	AMOUNT PAID	UNPAID BALANCE	NOTES
○						
○						
○						
○						
○						
○						
○						
○						
○						
○						
○						
○						
○						
○						
○						
○						
○						
○						
○						
○						
○						
○						
○						
○						
○						
TOTAL						

NOTES: _____

_____

_____

BILL PAYMENT  ORGANIZER

YEAR: .... MONTH: ....

PAID	BILL	DUE DATE	AMOUNT DUE	AMOUNT PAID	UNPAID BALANCE	NOTES
○						
○						
○						
○						
○						
○						
○						
○						
○						
○						
○						
○						
○						
○						
○						
○						
○						
○						
○						
○						
○						
○						
○						
○						
TOTAL						

NOTES: _____

_____

_____

BILL PAYMENT  ORGANIZER

YEAR: ....   **MONTH:** ....

PAID	BILL	DUE DATE	AMOUNT DUE	AMOUNT PAID	UNPAID BALANCE	NOTES
○						
○						
○						
○						
○						
○						
○						
○						
○						
○						
○						
○						
○						
○						
○						
○						
○						
○						
○						
○						
○						
○						
○						
○						
TOTAL						

NOTES: ....

....

....

BILL PAYMENT  ORGANIZER

YEAR: ....   **MONTH:** ....

PAID	BILL	DUE DATE	AMOUNT DUE	AMOUNT PAID	UNPAID BALANCE	NOTES
○						
○						
○						
○						
○						
○						
○						
○						
○						
○						
○						
○						
○						
○						
○						
○						
○						
○						
○						
○						
○						
○						
○						
○						
TOTAL						

NOTES: _____

_____

_____

BILL PAYMENT  ORGANIZER

YEAR: .... MONTH: ....

PAID	BILL	DUE DATE	AMOUNT DUE	AMOUNT PAID	UNPAID BALANCE	NOTES
○						
○						
○						
○						
○						
○						
○						
○						
○						
○						
○						
○						
○						
○						
○						
○						
○						
○						
○						
○						
○						
○						
○						
○						
TOTAL						

NOTES: _____

_____

_____

BILL PAYMENT ORGANIZER

YEAR: .... MONTH: ....

PAID	BILL	DUE DATE	AMOUNT DUE	AMOUNT PAID	UNPAID BALANCE	NOTES
○						
○						
○						
○						
○						
○						
○						
○						
○						
○						
○						
○						
○						
○						
○						
○						
○						
○						
○						
○						
○						
○						
○						
TOTAL						

NOTES: _____

_____

_____

BILL PAYMENT  ORGANIZER

YEAR: .... MONTH: ....

PAID	BILL	DUE DATE	AMOUNT DUE	AMOUNT PAID	UNPAID BALANCE	NOTES
○						
○						
○						
○						
○						
○						
○						
○						
○						
○						
○						
○						
○						
○						
○						
○						
○						
○						
○						
○						
○						
○						
○						
○						
TOTAL						

NOTES: _____

_____

_____

BILL PAYMENT  ORGANIZER

YEAR: .... **MONTH:** ....

PAID	BILL	DUE DATE	AMOUNT DUE	AMOUNT PAID	UNPAID BALANCE	NOTES
○						
○						
○						
○						
○						
○						
○						
○						
○						
○						
○						
○						
○						
○						
○						
○						
○						
○						
○						
○						
○						
○						
○						
○						
TOTAL						

NOTES: _____

_____

_____

BILL PAYMENT  ORGANIZER

YEAR: ....   **MONTH:** ....

PAID	BILL	DUE DATE	AMOUNT DUE	AMOUNT PAID	UNPAID BALANCE	NOTES
○						
○						
○						
○						
○						
○						
○						
○						
○						
○						
○						
○						
○						
○						
○						
○						
○						
○						
○						
○						
○						
○						
○						
TOTAL						

NOTES: _____

_____

_____

BILL PAYMENT  ORGANIZER

YEAR: ....   MONTH: ....

PAID	BILL	DUE DATE	AMOUNT DUE	AMOUNT PAID	UNPAID BALANCE	NOTES
○						
○						
○						
○						
○						
○						
○						
○						
○						
○						
○						
○						
○						
○						
○						
○						
○						
○						
○						
○						
○						
○						
○						
○						
TOTAL						

NOTES: _____

_____

_____

BILL PAYMENT  ORGANIZER

YEAR: .... **MONTH:** ....

PAID	BILL	DUE DATE	AMOUNT DUE	AMOUNT PAID	UNPAID BALANCE	NOTES
○						
○						
○						
○						
○						
○						
○						
○						
○						
○						
○						
○						
○						
○						
○						
○						
○						
○						
○						
○						
○						
○						
○						
○						
TOTAL						

NOTES: _____

_____

_____

BILL PAYMENT  ORGANIZER

YEAR: .... **MONTH:** ....

PAID	BILL	DUE DATE	AMOUNT DUE	AMOUNT PAID	UNPAID BALANCE	NOTES
○						
○						
○						
○						
○						
○						
○						
○						
○						
○						
○						
○						
○						
○						
○						
○						
○						
○						
○						
○						
○						
○						
○						
○						
TOTAL						

NOTES: _____

_____

_____

BILL PAYMENT ORGANIZER

YEAR: .... **MONTH:** ....

PAID	BILL	DUE DATE	AMOUNT DUE	AMOUNT PAID	UNPAID BALANCE	NOTES
○						
○						
○						
○						
○						
○						
○						
○						
○						
○						
○						
○						
○						
○						
○						
○						
○						
○						
○						
○						
○						
○						
○						
○						
TOTAL						

NOTES: _____

_____

_____

BILL PAYMENT ORGANIZER

YEAR: .... MONTH: ....

PAID	BILL	DUE DATE	AMOUNT DUE	AMOUNT PAID	UNPAID BALANCE	NOTES
○						
○						
○						
○						
○						
○						
○						
○						
○						
○						
○						
○						
○						
○						
○						
○						
○						
○						
○						
○						
○						
○						
○						
TOTAL						

NOTES: _____

_____

_____

BILL PAYMENT  ORGANIZER

YEAR: ....   MONTH: ....

PAID	BILL	DUE DATE	AMOUNT DUE	AMOUNT PAID	UNPAID BALANCE	NOTES
○						
○						
○						
○						
○						
○						
○						
○						
○						
○						
○						
○						
○						
○						
○						
○						
○						
○						
○						
○						
○						
○						
○						
○						
TOTAL						

NOTES: _____

_____

_____

BILL PAYMENT  ORGANIZER

YEAR: .... MONTH: ....

PAID	BILL	DUE DATE	AMOUNT DUE	AMOUNT PAID	UNPAID BALANCE	NOTES
○						
○						
○						
○						
○						
○						
○						
○						
○						
○						
○						
○						
○						
○						
○						
○						
○						
○						
○						
○						
○						
○						
○						
○						
○						
TOTAL						

NOTES: _____

_____

_____

BILL PAYMENT ORGANIZER

YEAR: _____   MONTH: _____

PAID	BILL	DUE DATE	AMOUNT DUE	AMOUNT PAID	UNPAID BALANCE	NOTES
○						
○						
○						
○						
○						
○						
○						
○						
○						
○						
○						
○						
○						
○						
○						
○						
○						
○						
○						
○						
○						
○						
○						
○						
○						
TOTAL						

NOTES: _____

_____

_____

BILL PAYMENT  ORGANIZER

YEAR: ....   **MONTH:** ....

PAID	BILL	DUE DATE	AMOUNT DUE	AMOUNT PAID	UNPAID BALANCE	NOTES
○						
○						
○						
○						
○						
○						
○						
○						
○						
○						
○						
○						
○						
○						
○						
○						
○						
○						
○						
○						
○						
○						
○						
○						
TOTAL						

NOTES: _____

_____

_____

BILL PAYMENT ORGANIZER

YEAR: ....   MONTH: ....

PAID	BILL	DUE DATE	AMOUNT DUE	AMOUNT PAID	UNPAID BALANCE	NOTES
○						
○						
○						
○						
○						
○						
○						
○						
○						
○						
○						
○						
○						
○						
○						
○						
○						
○						
○						
○						
○						
○						
○						
○						
TOTAL						

NOTES: _____

_____

_____

BILL PAYMENT  ORGANIZER

YEAR: .... MONTH: ....

PAID	BILL	DUE DATE	AMOUNT DUE	AMOUNT PAID	UNPAID BALANCE	NOTES
○						
○						
○						
○						
○						
○						
○						
○						
○						
○						
○						
○						
○						
○						
○						
○						
○						
○						
○						
○						
○						
○						
○						
○						
○						
TOTAL						

NOTES: _____

_____

_____

BILL PAYMENT ORGANIZER

YEAR: .... MONTH: ....

PAID	BILL	DUE DATE	AMOUNT DUE	AMOUNT PAID	UNPAID BALANCE	NOTES
○						
○						
○						
○						
○						
○						
○						
○						
○						
○						
○						
○						
○						
○						
○						
○						
○						
○						
○						
○						
○						
○						
○						
○						
○						
TOTAL						

NOTES: _____

_____

_____

BILL PAYMENT  ORGANIZER

YEAR: .... **MONTH:** ....

PAID	BILL	DUE DATE	AMOUNT DUE	AMOUNT PAID	UNPAID BALANCE	NOTES
○						
○						
○						
○						
○						
○						
○						
○						
○						
○						
○						
○						
○						
○						
○						
○						
○						
○						
○						
○						
○						
○						
○						
○						
TOTAL						

NOTES: _____

_____

_____

BILL PAYMENT  ORGANIZER

YEAR: ....   MONTH: ....

PAID	BILL	DUE DATE	AMOUNT DUE	AMOUNT PAID	UNPAID BALANCE	NOTES
○						
○						
○						
○						
○						
○						
○						
○						
○						
○						
○						
○						
○						
○						
○						
○						
○						
○						
○						
○						
○						
○						
○						
○						
○						
○						
TOTAL						

NOTES: _____

_____

_____

BILL PAYMENT  ORGANIZER

YEAR: .... **MONTH:** ....

PAID	BILL	DUE DATE	AMOUNT DUE	AMOUNT PAID	UNPAID BALANCE	NOTES
○						
○						
○						
○						
○						
○						
○						
○						
○						
○						
○						
○						
○						
○						
○						
○						
○						
○						
○						
○						
○						
○						
○						
○						
○						
TOTAL						

NOTES: _____

_____

_____

BILL PAYMENT  ORGANIZER

YEAR: _____   MONTH: _____

PAID	BILL	DUE DATE	AMOUNT DUE	AMOUNT PAID	UNPAID BALANCE	NOTES
○						
○						
○						
○						
○						
○						
○						
○						
○						
○						
○						
○						
○						
○						
○						
○						
○						
○						
○						
○						
○						
○						
○						
○						
○						
TOTAL						

NOTES: _____

_____

_____

BILL PAYMENT  ORGANIZER

YEAR: .... **MONTH:** ....

PAID	BILL	DUE DATE	AMOUNT DUE	AMOUNT PAID	UNPAID BALANCE	NOTES
○						
○						
○						
○						
○						
○						
○						
○						
○						
○						
○						
○						
○						
○						
○						
○						
○						
○						
○						
○						
○						
○						
○						
TOTAL						

NOTES: _____

_____

_____

BILL PAYMENT ORGANIZER

YEAR: ....   MONTH: ....

PAID	BILL	DUE DATE	AMOUNT DUE	AMOUNT PAID	UNPAID BALANCE	NOTES
○						
○						
○						
○						
○						
○						
○						
○						
○						
○						
○						
○						
○						
○						
○						
○						
○						
○						
○						
○						
○						
○						
○						
○						
○						
TOTAL						

NOTES: _____

_____

_____

BILL PAYMENT  ORGANIZER

YEAR: ....   MONTH: ....

PAID	BILL	DUE DATE	AMOUNT DUE	AMOUNT PAID	UNPAID BALANCE	NOTES
○						
○						
○						
○						
○						
○						
○						
○						
○						
○						
○						
○						
○						
○						
○						
○						
○						
○						
○						
○						
○						
○						
○						
○						
TOTAL						

NOTES: _____

_____

_____

BILL PAYMENT  ORGANIZER

YEAR: .... MONTH: ....

PAID	BILL	DUE DATE	AMOUNT DUE	AMOUNT PAID	UNPAID BALANCE	NOTES
○						
○						
○						
○						
○						
○						
○						
○						
○						
○						
○						
○						
○						
○						
○						
○						
○						
○						
○						
○						
○						
○						
○						
○						
○						
TOTAL						

NOTES: _____

_____

_____

BILL PAYMENT ORGANIZER

YEAR: .... MONTH: ....

PAID	BILL	DUE DATE	AMOUNT DUE	AMOUNT PAID	UNPAID BALANCE	NOTES
○						
○						
○						
○						
○						
○						
○						
○						
○						
○						
○						
○						
○						
○						
○						
○						
○						
○						
○						
○						
○						
○						
○						
○						
TOTAL						

NOTES: _____

_____

_____

BILL PAYMENT  ORGANIZER

YEAR: .... MONTH: ....

PAID	BILL	DUE DATE	AMOUNT DUE	AMOUNT PAID	UNPAID BALANCE	NOTES
○						
○						
○						
○						
○						
○						
○						
○						
○						
○						
○						
○						
○						
○						
○						
○						
○						
○						
○						
○						
○						
○						
○						
○						
TOTAL						

NOTES: _____

_____

_____

BILL PAYMENT  ORGANIZER

YEAR: ....   MONTH: ....

PAID	BILL	DUE DATE	AMOUNT DUE	AMOUNT PAID	UNPAID BALANCE	NOTES
○						
○						
○						
○						
○						
○						
○						
○						
○						
○						
○						
○						
○						
○						
○						
○						
○						
○						
○						
○						
○						
○						
○						
○						
○						
TOTAL						

NOTES: _____

_____

_____

BILL PAYMENT  ORGANIZER

YEAR: ....   MONTH: ....

PAID	BILL	DUE DATE	AMOUNT DUE	AMOUNT PAID	UNPAID BALANCE	NOTES
○						
○						
○						
○						
○						
○						
○						
○						
○						
○						
○						
○						
○						
○						
○						
○						
○						
○						
○						
○						
○						
○						
○						
○						
TOTAL						

NOTES: _____

_____

_____

BILL PAYMENT  ORGANIZER

YEAR: .... **MONTH:** ....

PAID	BILL	DUE DATE	AMOUNT DUE	AMOUNT PAID	UNPAID BALANCE	NOTES
○						
○						
○						
○						
○						
○						
○						
○						
○						
○						
○						
○						
○						
○						
○						
○						
○						
○						
○						
○						
○						
○						
○						
TOTAL						

NOTES: _____

_____

_____

BILL PAYMENT  ORGANIZER

YEAR: .... **MONTH:** ....

PAID	BILL	DUE DATE	AMOUNT DUE	AMOUNT PAID	UNPAID BALANCE	NOTES
○						
○						
○						
○						
○						
○						
○						
○						
○						
○						
○						
○						
○						
○						
○						
○						
○						
○						
○						
○						
○						
○						
○						
○						
TOTAL						

NOTES: _____

_____

_____

BILL PAYMENT  ORGANIZER

YEAR: .... MONTH: ....

PAID	BILL	DUE DATE	AMOUNT DUE	AMOUNT PAID	UNPAID BALANCE	NOTES
○						
○						
○						
○						
○						
○						
○						
○						
○						
○						
○						
○						
○						
○						
○						
○						
○						
○						
○						
○						
○						
○						
○						
TOTAL						

NOTES: _____

_____

_____

BILL PAYMENT  ORGANIZER

YEAR: ....   MONTH: ....

PAID	BILL	DUE DATE	AMOUNT DUE	AMOUNT PAID	UNPAID BALANCE	NOTES
○						
○						
○						
○						
○						
○						
○						
○						
○						
○						
○						
○						
○						
○						
○						
○						
○						
○						
○						
○						
○						
○						
○						
○						
TOTAL						

NOTES: _____

_____

_____

BILL PAYMENT  ORGANIZER

YEAR: ....   MONTH: ....

PAID	BILL	DUE DATE	AMOUNT DUE	AMOUNT PAID	UNPAID BALANCE	NOTES
○						
○						
○						
○						
○						
○						
○						
○						
○						
○						
○						
○						
○						
○						
○						
○						
○						
○						
○						
○						
○						
○						
○						
○						
TOTAL						

NOTES: _____

_____

_____

BILL PAYMENT  ORGANIZER

YEAR: .... 　　MONTH: ....

PAID	BILL	DUE DATE	AMOUNT DUE	AMOUNT PAID	UNPAID BALANCE	NOTES
○						
○						
○						
○						
○						
○						
○						
○						
○						
○						
○						
○						
○						
○						
○						
○						
○						
○						
○						
○						
○						
○						
○						
○						
TOTAL						

NOTES: _____

_____

_____

BILL PAYMENT  ORGANIZER

YEAR: ....   MONTH: ....

PAID	BILL	DUE DATE	AMOUNT DUE	AMOUNT PAID	UNPAID BALANCE	NOTES
◯						
◯						
◯						
◯						
◯						
◯						
◯						
◯						
◯						
◯						
◯						
◯						
◯						
◯						
◯						
◯						
◯						
◯						
◯						
◯						
◯						
◯						
◯						
◯						
◯						
TOTAL						

NOTES: _____

_____

_____

BILL PAYMENT  ORGANIZER

YEAR: _____   MONTH: _____

PAID	BILL	DUE DATE	AMOUNT DUE	AMOUNT PAID	UNPAID BALANCE	NOTES
○						
○						
○						
○						
○						
○						
○						
○						
○						
○						
○						
○						
○						
○						
○						
○						
○						
○						
○						
○						
○						
○						
○						
○						
○						
TOTAL						

NOTES: _____

_____

_____

BILL PAYMENT  ORGANIZER

YEAR: .... MONTH: ....

PAID	BILL	DUE DATE	AMOUNT DUE	AMOUNT PAID	UNPAID BALANCE	NOTES
○						
○						
○						
○						
○						
○						
○						
○						
○						
○						
○						
○						
○						
○						
○						
○						
○						
○						
○						
○						
○						
○						
○						
TOTAL						

NOTES: _____

_____

_____

BILL PAYMENT  ORGANIZER

YEAR: .... **MONTH:** ....

PAID	BILL	DUE DATE	AMOUNT DUE	AMOUNT PAID	UNPAID BALANCE	NOTES
○						
○						
○						
○						
○						
○						
○						
○						
○						
○						
○						
○						
○						
○						
○						
○						
○						
○						
○						
○						
○						
○						
○						
TOTAL						

NOTES: _____

_____

_____

BILL PAYMENT  ORGANIZER

YEAR: .... MONTH: ....

PAID	BILL	DUE DATE	AMOUNT DUE	AMOUNT PAID	UNPAID BALANCE	NOTES
○						
○						
○						
○						
○						
○						
○						
○						
○						
○						
○						
○						
○						
○						
○						
○						
○						
○						
○						
○						
○						
○						
○						
○						
TOTAL						

NOTES: _____

_____

_____

BILL PAYMENT  ORGANIZER

YEAR: .... MONTH: ....

PAID	BILL	DUE DATE	AMOUNT DUE	AMOUNT PAID	UNPAID BALANCE	NOTES
○						
○						
○						
○						
○						
○						
○						
○						
○						
○						
○						
○						
○						
○						
○						
○						
○						
○						
○						
○						
○						
○						
○						
○						
TOTAL						

NOTES: _____

_____

_____

BILL PAYMENT  ORGANIZER

YEAR: .... **MONTH:** ....

PAID	BILL	DUE DATE	AMOUNT DUE	AMOUNT PAID	UNPAID BALANCE	NOTES
○						
○						
○						
○						
○						
○						
○						
○						
○						
○						
○						
○						
○						
○						
○						
○						
○						
○						
○						
○						
○						
○						
○						
○						
TOTAL						

NOTES: _____

_____

BILL PAYMENT  ORGANIZER

YEAR: .... **MONTH:** ....

PAID	BILL	DUE DATE	AMOUNT DUE	AMOUNT PAID	UNPAID BALANCE	NOTES
○						
○						
○						
○						
○						
○						
○						
○						
○						
○						
○						
○						
○						
○						
○						
○						
○						
○						
○						
○						
○						
○						
○						
○						
TOTAL						

NOTES: _____

_____

_____

BILL PAYMENT  ORGANIZER

YEAR: ....   MONTH: ....

PAID	BILL	DUE DATE	AMOUNT DUE	AMOUNT PAID	UNPAID BALANCE	NOTES
○						
○						
○						
○						
○						
○						
○						
○						
○						
○						
○						
○						
○						
○						
○						
○						
○						
○						
○						
○						
○						
○						
○						
○						
TOTAL						

NOTES: _____

_____

_____

BILL PAYMENT  ORGANIZER

YEAR: .... **MONTH:** ....

PAID	BILL	DUE DATE	AMOUNT DUE	AMOUNT PAID	UNPAID BALANCE	NOTES
○						
○						
○						
○						
○						
○						
○						
○						
○						
○						
○						
○						
○						
○						
○						
○						
○						
○						
○						
○						
○						
○						
○						
TOTAL						

NOTES: _____

_____

_____

BILL PAYMENT  ORGANIZER

YEAR: _____   **MONTH:** _____

PAID	BILL	DUE DATE	AMOUNT DUE	AMOUNT PAID	UNPAID BALANCE	NOTES
○						
○						
○						
○						
○						
○						
○						
○						
○						
○						
○						
○						
○						
○						
○						
○						
○						
○						
○						
○						
○						
○						
○						
○						
TOTAL						

NOTES: _____

_____

_____

BILL PAYMENT  ORGANIZER

YEAR: ....   MONTH: ....

PAID	BILL	DUE DATE	AMOUNT DUE	AMOUNT PAID	UNPAID BALANCE	NOTES
○						
○						
○						
○						
○						
○						
○						
○						
○						
○						
○						
○						
○						
○						
○						
○						
○						
○						
○						
○						
○						
○						
○						
○						
○						
TOTAL						

NOTES: ———————————————————————————————
———————————————————————————————————
———————————————————————————————————

BILL PAYMENT  ORGANIZER

YEAR: .... **MONTH:** ....

PAID	BILL	DUE DATE	AMOUNT DUE	AMOUNT PAID	UNPAID BALANCE	NOTES
○						
○						
○						
○						
○						
○						
○						
○						
○						
○						
○						
○						
○						
○						
○						
○						
○						
○						
○						
○						
○						
○						
○						
○						
○						
TOTAL						

NOTES: _____

_____

_____

BILL PAYMENT  ORGANIZER

YEAR: .... **MONTH:** ....

PAID	BILL	DUE DATE	AMOUNT DUE	AMOUNT PAID	UNPAID BALANCE	NOTES
○						
○						
○						
○						
○						
○						
○						
○						
○						
○						
○						
○						
○						
○						
○						
○						
○						
○						
○						
○						
○						
○						
○						
○						
TOTAL						

NOTES: _____

_____

_____

BILL PAYMENT ORGANIZER

YEAR: .... MONTH: ....

PAID	BILL	DUE DATE	AMOUNT DUE	AMOUNT PAID	UNPAID BALANCE	NOTES
○						
○						
○						
○						
○						
○						
○						
○						
○						
○						
○						
○						
○						
○						
○						
○						
○						
○						
○						
○						
○						
○						
○						
○						
TOTAL						

NOTES: _____

_____

_____

BILL PAYMENT  ORGANIZER

YEAR: .... MONTH: ....

PAID	BILL	DUE DATE	AMOUNT DUE	AMOUNT PAID	UNPAID BALANCE	NOTES
○						
○						
○						
○						
○						
○						
○						
○						
○						
○						
○						
○						
○						
○						
○						
○						
○						
○						
○						
○						
○						
○						
○						
○						
TOTAL						

NOTES: _____

_____

_____

BILL PAYMENT  ORGANIZER

YEAR: .... MONTH: ....

PAID	BILL	DUE DATE	AMOUNT DUE	AMOUNT PAID	UNPAID BALANCE	NOTES
○						
○						
○						
○						
○						
○						
○						
○						
○						
○						
○						
○						
○						
○						
○						
○						
○						
○						
○						
○						
○						
○						
○						
○						
○						
TOTAL						

NOTES: _____

_____

_____

BILL PAYMENT  ORGANIZER

YEAR: .... **MONTH:** ....

PAID	BILL	DUE DATE	AMOUNT DUE	AMOUNT PAID	UNPAID BALANCE	NOTES
○						
○						
○						
○						
○						
○						
○						
○						
○						
○						
○						
○						
○						
○						
○						
○						
○						
○						
○						
○						
○						
○						
○						
○						
TOTAL						

NOTES: ....
....
....

BILL PAYMENT  ORGANIZER

YEAR: .... MONTH: ....

PAID	BILL	DUE DATE	AMOUNT DUE	AMOUNT PAID	UNPAID BALANCE	NOTES
○						
○						
○						
○						
○						
○						
○						
○						
○						
○						
○						
○						
○						
○						
○						
○						
○						
○						
○						
○						
○						
○						
○						
TOTAL						

NOTES: _____

_____

_____

BILL PAYMENT  ORGANIZER

YEAR: ....   **MONTH:** ....

PAID	BILL	DUE DATE	AMOUNT DUE	AMOUNT PAID	UNPAID BALANCE	NOTES
○						
○						
○						
○						
○						
○						
○						
○						
○						
○						
○						
○						
○						
○						
○						
○						
○						
○						
○						
○						
○						
○						
○						
○						
TOTAL						

NOTES: ————————————————————————————————————

————————————————————————————————————

————————————————————————————————————

BILL PAYMENT ORGANIZER

YEAR: .... **MONTH:** ....

PAID	BILL	DUE DATE	AMOUNT DUE	AMOUNT PAID	UNPAID BALANCE	NOTES
○						
○						
○						
○						
○						
○						
○						
○						
○						
○						
○						
○						
○						
○						
○						
○						
○						
○						
○						
○						
○						
○						
○						
○						
○						
TOTAL						

NOTES: _____

_____

_____

BILL PAYMENT  ORGANIZER

YEAR: .... MONTH: ....

PAID	BILL	DUE DATE	AMOUNT DUE	AMOUNT PAID	UNPAID BALANCE	NOTES
○						
○						
○						
○						
○						
○						
○						
○						
○						
○						
○						
○						
○						
○						
○						
○						
○						
○						
○						
○						
○						
○						
○						
○						
○						
TOTAL						

NOTES: _____

_____

_____

BILL PAYMENT  ORGANIZER

YEAR: .... **MONTH:** ....

PAID	BILL	DUE DATE	AMOUNT DUE	AMOUNT PAID	UNPAID BALANCE	NOTES
○						
○						
○						
○						
○						
○						
○						
○						
○						
○						
○						
○						
○						
○						
○						
○						
○						
○						
○						
○						
○						
○						
○						
○						
TOTAL						

NOTES: _____

_____

_____

BILL PAYMENT  ORGANIZER

PAID	BILL	DUE DATE	AMOUNT DUE	AMOUNT PAID	UNPAID BALANCE	NOTES
○						
○						
○						
○						
○						
○						
○						
○						
○						
○						
○						
○						
○						
○						
○						
○						
○						
○						
○						
○						
○						
○						
○						
○						
○						
○						
TOTAL						

NOTES: _____

_____

_____

BILL PAYMENT  ORGANIZER

YEAR: .... **MONTH:** ....

PAID	BILL	DUE DATE	AMOUNT DUE	AMOUNT PAID	UNPAID BALANCE	NOTES
○						
○						
○						
○						
○						
○						
○						
○						
○						
○						
○						
○						
○						
○						
○						
○						
○						
○						
○						
○						
○						
○						
○						
○						
TOTAL						

NOTES: _____

_____

_____

BILL PAYMENT  ORGANIZER

YEAR: ....   MONTH: ....

PAID	BILL	DUE DATE	AMOUNT DUE	AMOUNT PAID	UNPAID BALANCE	NOTES
○						
○						
○						
○						
○						
○						
○						
○						
○						
○						
○						
○						
○						
○						
○						
○						
○						
○						
○						
○						
○						
○						
○						
○						
○						
TOTAL						

NOTES: _____

_____

_____

BILL PAYMENT  ORGANIZER

YEAR: ....   **MONTH:** ....

PAID	BILL	DUE DATE	AMOUNT DUE	AMOUNT PAID	UNPAID BALANCE	NOTES
○						
○						
○						
○						
○						
○						
○						
○						
○						
○						
○						
○						
○						
○						
○						
○						
○						
○						
○						
○						
○						
○						
○						
○						
TOTAL						

NOTES: _____

_____

_____

BILL PAYMENT  ORGANIZER

YEAR: ....   MONTH: ....

PAID	BILL	DUE DATE	AMOUNT DUE	AMOUNT PAID	UNPAID BALANCE	NOTES
○						
○						
○						
○						
○						
○						
○						
○						
○						
○						
○						
○						
○						
○						
○						
○						
○						
○						
○						
○						
○						
○						
○						
○						
TOTAL						

NOTES: _____

_____

_____

BILL PAYMENT  ORGANIZER

YEAR: ....   **MONTH:** ....

PAID	BILL	DUE DATE	AMOUNT DUE	AMOUNT PAID	UNPAID BALANCE	NOTES
○						
○						
○						
○						
○						
○						
○						
○						
○						
○						
○						
○						
○						
○						
○						
○						
○						
○						
○						
○						
○						
○						
○						
○						
○						
TOTAL						

NOTES: _____

_____

_____

BILL PAYMENT  ORGANIZER

YEAR: .... **MONTH:** ....

PAID	BILL	DUE DATE	AMOUNT DUE	AMOUNT PAID	UNPAID BALANCE	NOTES
○						
○						
○						
○						
○						
○						
○						
○						
○						
○						
○						
○						
○						
○						
○						
○						
○						
○						
○						
○						
○						
○						
○						
○						
TOTAL						

NOTES: _____

_____

_____

BILL PAYMENT  ORGANIZER

YEAR: .... **MONTH:** ....

PAID	BILL	DUE DATE	AMOUNT DUE	AMOUNT PAID	UNPAID BALANCE	NOTES
○						
○						
○						
○						
○						
○						
○						
○						
○						
○						
○						
○						
○						
○						
○						
○						
○						
○						
○						
○						
○						
○						
○						
○						
○						
TOTAL						

NOTES: _____

_____

_____

BILL PAYMENT ORGANIZER

YEAR: .... MONTH: ....

PAID	BILL	DUE DATE	AMOUNT DUE	AMOUNT PAID	UNPAID BALANCE	NOTES
○						
○						
○						
○						
○						
○						
○						
○						
○						
○						
○						
○						
○						
○						
○						
○						
○						
○						
○						
○						
○						
○						
○						
○						
TOTAL						

NOTES: _____

_____

_____

BILL PAYMENT  ORGANIZER

YEAR: ....   **MONTH:** ....

PAID	BILL	DUE DATE	AMOUNT DUE	AMOUNT PAID	UNPAID BALANCE	NOTES
○						
○						
○						
○						
○						
○						
○						
○						
○						
○						
○						
○						
○						
○						
○						
○						
○						
○						
○						
○						
○						
○						
○						
○						
TOTAL						

NOTES: _____

_____

_____

BILL PAYMENT  ORGANIZER

YEAR: .... **MONTH:** ....

PAID	BILL	DUE DATE	AMOUNT DUE	AMOUNT PAID	UNPAID BALANCE	NOTES
○						
○						
○						
○						
○						
○						
○						
○						
○						
○						
○						
○						
○						
○						
○						
○						
○						
○						
○						
○						
○						
○						
○						
○						
TOTAL						

NOTES: _____

_____

_____

BILL PAYMENT ORGANIZER

YEAR: ....   **MONTH:** ....

PAID	BILL	DUE DATE	AMOUNT DUE	AMOUNT PAID	UNPAID BALANCE	NOTES
○						
○						
○						
○						
○						
○						
○						
○						
○						
○						
○						
○						
○						
○						
○						
○						
○						
○						
○						
○						
○						
○						
○						
○						
TOTAL						

NOTES: _____

_____

_____

BILL PAYMENT  ORGANIZER

YEAR: ....   **MONTH:** ....

PAID	BILL	DUE DATE	AMOUNT DUE	AMOUNT PAID	UNPAID BALANCE	NOTES
○						
○						
○						
○						
○						
○						
○						
○						
○						
○						
○						
○						
○						
○						
○						
○						
○						
○						
○						
○						
○						
○						
○						
○						
TOTAL						

NOTES: _____

_____

_____

BILL PAYMENT  ORGANIZER

YEAR: ....   **MONTH:** ....

PAID	BILL	DUE DATE	AMOUNT DUE	AMOUNT PAID	UNPAID BALANCE	NOTES
○						
○						
○						
○						
○						
○						
○						
○						
○						
○						
○						
○						
○						
○						
○						
○						
○						
○						
○						
○						
○						
○						
○						
○						
○						
TOTAL						

NOTES: _____

_____

_____

BILL PAYMENT  ORGANIZER

YEAR: ....   **MONTH:** ....

PAID	BILL	DUE DATE	AMOUNT DUE	AMOUNT PAID	UNPAID BALANCE	NOTES
○						
○						
○						
○						
○						
○						
○						
○						
○						
○						
○						
○						
○						
○						
○						
○						
○						
○						
○						
○						
○						
○						
○						
○						
TOTAL						

NOTES: _____

_____

_____

BILL PAYMENT  ORGANIZER

YEAR: ....   MONTH: ....

PAID	BILL	DUE DATE	AMOUNT DUE	AMOUNT PAID	UNPAID BALANCE	NOTES
○						
○						
○						
○						
○						
○						
○						
○						
○						
○						
○						
○						
○						
○						
○						
○						
○						
○						
○						
○						
○						
○						
○						
○						
○						
TOTAL						

NOTES: _____

_____

_____

BILL PAYMENT  ORGANIZER

YEAR: .... MONTH: ....

PAID	BILL	DUE DATE	AMOUNT DUE	AMOUNT PAID	UNPAID BALANCE	NOTES
○						
○						
○						
○						
○						
○						
○						
○						
○						
○						
○						
○						
○						
○						
○						
○						
○						
○						
○						
○						
○						
○						
○						
○						
TOTAL						

NOTES: _____

_____

_____

BILL PAYMENT  ORGANIZER

YEAR: .... MONTH: ....

PAID	BILL	DUE DATE	AMOUNT DUE	AMOUNT PAID	UNPAID BALANCE	NOTES
○						
○						
○						
○						
○						
○						
○						
○						
○						
○						
○						
○						
○						
○						
○						
○						
○						
○						
○						
○						
○						
○						
○						
○						
TOTAL						

NOTES: _____

_____

_____

BILL PAYMENT  ORGANIZER

YEAR: ....   MONTH: ....

PAID	BILL	DUE DATE	AMOUNT DUE	AMOUNT PAID	UNPAID BALANCE	NOTES
○						
○						
○						
○						
○						
○						
○						
○						
○						
○						
○						
○						
○						
○						
○						
○						
○						
○						
○						
○						
○						
○						
○						
○						
○						
TOTAL						

NOTES: _____

_____

_____

BILL PAYMENT  ORGANIZER

YEAR: ....

MONTH: ....

PAID	BILL	DUE DATE	AMOUNT DUE	AMOUNT PAID	UNPAID BALANCE	NOTES
○						
○						
○						
○						
○						
○						
○						
○						
○						
○						
○						
○						
○						
○						
○						
○						
○						
○						
○						
○						
○						
○						
○						
○						
○						
TOTAL						

NOTES: _____

_____

_____

BILL PAYMENT  ORGANIZER

YEAR: .... **MONTH:** ....

PAID	BILL	DUE DATE	AMOUNT DUE	AMOUNT PAID	UNPAID BALANCE	NOTES
○						
○						
○						
○						
○						
○						
○						
○						
○						
○						
○						
○						
○						
○						
○						
○						
○						
○						
○						
○						
○						
○						
○						
○						
○						
TOTAL						

NOTES: _____

_____

_____

BILL PAYMENT  ORGANIZER

YEAR: .... **MONTH:** ....

PAID	BILL	DUE DATE	AMOUNT DUE	AMOUNT PAID	UNPAID BALANCE	NOTES
◯						
◯						
◯						
◯						
◯						
◯						
◯						
◯						
◯						
◯						
◯						
◯						
◯						
◯						
◯						
◯						
◯						
◯						
◯						
◯						
◯						
◯						
◯						
◯						
TOTAL						

NOTES: _____

_____

_____

BILL PAYMENT ORGANIZER

YEAR: .... MONTH: ....

PAID	BILL	DUE DATE	AMOUNT DUE	AMOUNT PAID	UNPAID BALANCE	NOTES
○						
○						
○						
○						
○						
○						
○						
○						
○						
○						
○						
○						
○						
○						
○						
○						
○						
○						
○						
○						
○						
○						
○						
○						
TOTAL						

NOTES: _____

_____

_____

BILL PAYMENT  ORGANIZER

YEAR: _____   MONTH: _____

PAID	BILL	DUE DATE	AMOUNT DUE	AMOUNT PAID	UNPAID BALANCE	NOTES
○						
○						
○						
○						
○						
○						
○						
○						
○						
○						
○						
○						
○						
○						
○						
○						
○						
○						
○						
○						
○						
○						
○						
○						
TOTAL						

NOTES: _____
_____
_____

BILL PAYMENT  ORGANIZER

YEAR: .... MONTH: ....

PAID	BILL	DUE DATE	AMOUNT DUE	AMOUNT PAID	UNPAID BALANCE	NOTES
○						
○						
○						
○						
○						
○						
○						
○						
○						
○						
○						
○						
○						
○						
○						
○						
○						
○						
○						
○						
○						
○						
○						
○						
TOTAL						

NOTES: _____

_____

_____

BILL PAYMENT  ORGANIZER

YEAR: ....   MONTH: ....

PAID	BILL	DUE DATE	AMOUNT DUE	AMOUNT PAID	UNPAID BALANCE	NOTES
○						
○						
○						
○						
○						
○						
○						
○						
○						
○						
○						
○						
○						
○						
○						
○						
○						
○						
○						
○						
○						
○						
○						
○						
TOTAL						

NOTES: _____
_____
_____

BILL PAYMENT  ORGANIZER

YEAR: .... MONTH: ....

PAID	BILL	DUE DATE	AMOUNT DUE	AMOUNT PAID	UNPAID BALANCE	NOTES
○						
○						
○						
○						
○						
○						
○						
○						
○						
○						
○						
○						
○						
○						
○						
○						
○						
○						
○						
○						
○						
○						
○						
○						
○						
TOTAL						

NOTES: _____

_____

_____

BILL PAYMENT  ORGANIZER

YEAR: ....   **MONTH:** ....

PAID	BILL	DUE DATE	AMOUNT DUE	AMOUNT PAID	UNPAID BALANCE	NOTES
○						
○						
○						
○						
○						
○						
○						
○						
○						
○						
○						
○						
○						
○						
○						
○						
○						
○						
○						
○						
○						
○						
○						
○						
TOTAL						

NOTES: _____

_____

_____

BILL PAYMENT  ORGANIZER

YEAR: ....   **MONTH:** ....

PAID	BILL	DUE DATE	AMOUNT DUE	AMOUNT PAID	UNPAID BALANCE	NOTES
○						
○						
○						
○						
○						
○						
○						
○						
○						
○						
○						
○						
○						
○						
○						
○						
○						
○						
○						
○						
○						
○						
○						
○						
○						
TOTAL						

NOTES: ——————————————————————————————————————

——

——

BILL PAYMENT  ORGANIZER

YEAR: .... MONTH: ....

PAID	BILL	DUE DATE	AMOUNT DUE	AMOUNT PAID	UNPAID BALANCE	NOTES
○						
○						
○						
○						
○						
○						
○						
○						
○						
○						
○						
○						
○						
○						
○						
○						
○						
○						
○						
○						
○						
○						
○						
○						
TOTAL						

NOTES: _____

_____

_____

BILL PAYMENT  ORGANIZER

YEAR: .... **MONTH:** ....

PAID	BILL	DUE DATE	AMOUNT DUE	AMOUNT PAID	UNPAID BALANCE	NOTES
○						
○						
○						
○						
○						
○						
○						
○						
○						
○						
○						
○						
○						
○						
○						
○						
○						
○						
○						
○						
○						
○						
○						
○						
○						
TOTAL						

NOTES: _____

_____

_____

BILL PAYMENT  ORGANIZER

YEAR: .... MONTH: ....

PAID	BILL	DUE DATE	AMOUNT DUE	AMOUNT PAID	UNPAID BALANCE	NOTES
○						
○						
○						
○						
○						
○						
○						
○						
○						
○						
○						
○						
○						
○						
○						
○						
○						
○						
○						
○						
○						
○						
○						
○						
○						
TOTAL						

NOTES: _____

_____

_____

BILL PAYMENT  ORGANIZER

YEAR: ....   MONTH: ....

PAID	BILL	DUE DATE	AMOUNT DUE	AMOUNT PAID	UNPAID BALANCE	NOTES
○						
○						
○						
○						
○						
○						
○						
○						
○						
○						
○						
○						
○						
○						
○						
○						
○						
○						
○						
○						
○						
○						
○						
TOTAL						

NOTES: _____

_____

_____

BILL PAYMENT  ORGANIZER

YEAR: .... **MONTH:** ....

PAID	BILL	DUE DATE	AMOUNT DUE	AMOUNT PAID	UNPAID BALANCE	NOTES
○						
○						
○						
○						
○						
○						
○						
○						
○						
○						
○						
○						
○						
○						
○						
○						
○						
○						
○						
○						
○						
○						
○						
○						
○						
TOTAL						

NOTES: ——————————————————————————————

_____

_____

BILL PAYMENT  ORGANIZER

YEAR: ....   **MONTH:** ....

PAID	BILL	DUE DATE	AMOUNT DUE	AMOUNT PAID	UNPAID BALANCE	NOTES
○						
○						
○						
○						
○						
○						
○						
○						
○						
○						
○						
○						
○						
○						
○						
○						
○						
○						
○						
○						
○						
○						
○						
○						
TOTAL						

NOTES: _____

_____

_____

BILL PAYMENT  ORGANIZER

YEAR: ....   MONTH: ....

PAID	BILL	DUE DATE	AMOUNT DUE	AMOUNT PAID	UNPAID BALANCE	NOTES
○						
○						
○						
○						
○						
○						
○						
○						
○						
○						
○						
○						
○						
○						
○						
○						
○						
○						
○						
○						
○						
○						
○						
○						
○						
TOTAL						

NOTES: _____

_____

_____

BILL PAYMENT  ORGANIZER

YEAR: ....   MONTH: ....

PAID	BILL	DUE DATE	AMOUNT DUE	AMOUNT PAID	UNPAID BALANCE	NOTES
○						
○						
○						
○						
○						
○						
○						
○						
○						
○						
○						
○						
○						
○						
○						
○						
○						
○						
○						
○						
○						
○						
○						
○						
○						
TOTAL						

NOTES: _____

_____

_____

Made in the USA
Monee, IL
05 January 2025

75979783R00070